Pets: The Hidden Costs of Companionship - Rethinking Ownership in Modern Society

Examining the Societal, Health, and Environmental Burdens of Pet Keeping

Marko Vovk

Copyright © 2024 by Marko Vovk

All rights reserved.

No portion of this book may be reproduced without written permission from the publisher or author except as permitted by U.S. copyright law.

This publication is designed to provide accurate and authoritative information regarding the subject matter covered. It is sold with the understanding that neither the author nor the publisher is engaged in rendering legal.

For permissions requests: Fixyourtoxichome.com

Paperback: ISBN: 979-8-9914055-2-2

Ebook::   ISBN: 979-8-9914055-3-9

Cover Design by Marko Vovk

Book Edit: Non-Human: (Autocrit, Word, Addicus, Perplexity, Grammarly Plus, Book Brush, Word Art)

Interior Design by Marko Vovk   Book Cover by Marko Vovk

Final Edit by Marko Vovk (Some minor inconsistencies may exist)   Printed in USA

Introduction

In recent decades, indoor pet ownership has transformed from a simple companionship to a complex phenomenon. This book comprehensively explores the multifaceted world of pet ownership, its evolution, its impact, and what's to come. From the rise of indoor pets to the environmental consequences of our furry friends, we examine the concealed costs and unexpected difficulties of intermingling animals into our homes and lives.

We'll uncover the health threats, both positive and negative, of living with pets. We will investigate the psychological effects of our bonds with animals and how it changes our lives. The book will cover indoor air conditions, parasites, worms, and zoonotic diseases. We will examine how much time is involved in feeding and caring for pets and the economic burden of pet care. We will learn about the legal complexities of this company ownership.

At the end of the book, we will know if we are benefiting from these indoor fury family members or if we have unwittingly created new problems. This book isn't just for pet owners. It's for anyone interested in understanding how our indoor pets affect our well-being, mindset, finances, and lives.

Contents

1. The Evolution of Pet Ownership — 1
2. The Rise of Indoor Pets — 5
3. The Hidden Dangers of Indoor Pets — 8
4. Parasites and Worms from Dogs — 13
5. Cats and Toxoplasma Gondii — 16
6. Zoonotic Diseases — 19
7. Wildlife and Health: The Hidden Dangers in Our Homes — 23
8. The Economic Burden of Pet Ownership — 26
9. Pets and Stress — 30
10. Dangerous Animals in the Home — 33
11. The Future of Pet Ownership — 36
12. Health Implications of Changing Homes along with Modern Pet Ownership — 40
13. Psychological Effects of Pet Ownership — 43

14. The Perpetual Toddler: Life with Pets   46
15. Final Words   50
16. Bibligrapjuy   54

Chapter 1

The Evolution of Pet Ownership

Pet ownership in the United States has transformed over the past century, reflecting broader changes and evolving human-animal relationships. This shift is characterized by a dramatic increase in indoor pet ownership, changing perceptions of pets' roles, and the growth of a multi-billion dollar pet industry.

In 1900, less than 5% of American households had indoor pets, with animals serving utilitarian purposes on farms and urban areas. By 1950, indoor pet ownership rose to 20% as urbanization increased. The 1980s saw a significant surge, with around 50% of households keeping pets indoors. In 2024, an estimated 70% of U.S. households own pets, with the majority residing indoors.

The 1960s marked a transitional period, with many families still maintaining outdoor dog houses, a practice that declined in subsequent decades. As people moved to cities, they brought animals indoors, transforming their roles from working animals to companions. This shift was driven by changing family structures, increased loneliness in urban settings, and growing recognition of the emotional benefits of pet ownership.

Today, 66% of U.S. households (86.9 million homes) own a pet, up from 56% in 1988. Dogs remain the most popular pet, with 66 million households owning at least one, followed by cats in 47 million households. The total number of dogs in the United States is 90 million, while cats are 63 million.

The pet industry has grown, with total expenditures reaching $147 billion in 2023, up 7.5% from 2022. Pet insurance has also gained popularity, with 5.7 million pets insured in the U.S. by the end of 2023. Millennials make up the most significant percentage of current pet owners (33%), followed by Gen X (25%) and baby boomers (24%).

Pet ownership varies by income and location, with higher-income households and rural residents more likely to own pets. The costs associated with pet ownership can be substantial, with dog owners spending an average of $2,524 yearly while cat owners spend about $1,200 yearly. These costs accumulate over a pet's lifetime, reflecting the financial commitment involved in pet ownership. So, if you have a ten-year-old dog, the accrued cost could be over $25,000.

The growing trend of integrating pets into households brings important considerations beyond companionship. As pets become central to family life, issues like indoor air quality, zoonotic diseases, and environmental impacts must be addressed.

Chapter 2

The Rise of Indoor Pets

The time investment in pet care is substantial. On average, pet owners spend 0.77 hours (46 minutes) daily with their pets, which amounts to 281 hours over a year. For a pet's average lifespan of 13 years, owners dedicate five months. This time commitment represents a significant portion of an individual's life, impacting other activities and relationships.

Financial expenditures on pets have risen. Americans spent $136.8 billion on their pets in 2022, a 10.68 % increase from 2021. Essential dog expenses average $1,533 per year. Over a 13-year lifespan, this totals $19,929, not accounting for inflation or unexpected costs.

The "opportunity cost" of pet ownership extends beyond finances. Time spent with pets could be used for personal development, career advancement, or nurturing human relationships. For example, the 281 hours spent annually on pet care could equate to learning a new language, completing a part-time course, or dedicating more time to family and friends.

Pet ownership can affect human relationships in various ways. Some individuals prioritize their pets over social engagements, leading to missed opportunities for human connection. For instance, 38% of pet owners have gone into debt for their pets, which could strain relationships with partners or family members who don't share the same priorities.

The rise of "pet parents" has led to a shift in family dynamics. Sometimes, couples choose pets over children, contributing to declining birth rates. This trend can create generational gaps and alter family structures.

Most pet owners (33%) are millennials, often treating their pets as surrogate children. This can reduce the time and resources needed to build and maintain human relationships. For example, the average $2,524 annual spending on dogs could otherwise fund several date nights or family outings.

The time devoted to pets can also limit spontaneity in relationships. Vacation planning becomes more complex, with 26.7% of pet owners citing veterinary care as their most significant expense. This can restrict travel opportunities and strain relationships with non-pet-owning friends or partners.

Chapter 3

The Hidden Dangers of Indoor Pets

The rise of indoor pet ownership brings unexpected consequences for home environments and human health. Pets produce particulate matter through shedding, dander, saliva, and fecal elements, contributing to indoor air pollution. These particles become airborne, settling on surfaces and circulating through ventilation systems, impacting air quality throughout the home.

As homes become more energy-efficient and airtight, indoor air pollution intensifies. Reduced air exchange traps contaminants, creating an ideal environment for dust mites to thrive. Dust mites feed on pet dander and human skin cells, multiplying in warm, humid conditions.

An average mattress contains 100,000 to 10 million dust mites, and a typical pillow houses 1 million. These microscopic arachnids produce waste that triggers allergic reactions, contributing to indoor allergen levels and exacerbating respiratory issues in sensitive individuals.

The correlation between indoor pets and respiratory problems has grown over the past century. In 1900, asthma affected less than 1% of children in the United States. By 1950, this rate increased to 2-3%, coinciding with the trend of keeping pets indoors.

The 1990s saw a sharp rise in childhood asthma rates, reaching 7.5% of children. In 2024, 8.4% of children in the U.S. have asthma. This increase parallels the growth in indoor pet ownership and time spent in sealed environments.

Allergies have followed a similar trajectory. In the early 1900s, allergies were rare, affecting less than 1% of the population. By 1950, allergy rates climbed to 5-10%. In the 1990s, 20-25% of Americans reported allergies.

Today, over 30% of adults and 40% of children in the U.S. suffer from allergies. The prevalence of indoor pets, with pet dander being a common allergen, contributes to this trend. Respiratory issues, including chronic bronchitis and sinusitis, have also increased.

Modern construction techniques and energy conservation efforts have led to tighter home environments. While beneficial for energy efficiency, these sealed spaces trap pollutants, including pet-related particulates. Reduced air exchange exacerbates the concentration of allergens and irritants. Combining tighter homes and increased pet ownership creates a perfect storm for indoor air quality issues. Pet dander, dust mites, and other allergens circulate in these sealed environments, leading to various health problems.

Exposure to pet-related indoor air pollution can result in various illnesses. Allergic rhinitis, characterized by sneezing, congestion, and itchy eyes, affects millions of Americans. Chronic sinusitis, often triggered by pet allergens, impacts 11% of U.S. adults.

Asthma exacerbations are common in homes with pets for children. Pet-induced asthma attacks can be severe, leading to hospitalizations and long-term lung damage. Chronic obstructive pulmonary disease (COPD) risk increases with prolonged exposure to pet-related air pollution.

Skin conditions, such as atopic dermatitis, can be triggered or worsened by pet allergens. Eczema rates have doubled since the 1970s, coinciding with increased indoor pet ownership. Pet-related particulates can also exacerbate existing skin conditions.

Zoonotic diseases, transmitted from pets to humans, pose additional risks in sealed homes. These include parasitic infections like toxoplasmosis from cats and various bacterial infections. Proximity to pets in confined spaces increases transmission likelihood.

Indoor air pollution from pets can impact cardiovascular health. Delicate particulate matter from pet dander and associated dust can penetrate the lungs and enter the bloodstream, contributing to inflammation and an increased risk of heart disease. Long-term exposure to poor indoor air quality may also affect cognitive function. Studies suggest a link between air pollution and cognitive decline, with implications for children's development and adult brain health. Pet-related pollutants contribute to this overall burden.

The impact of indoor pets extends beyond physical health. Mental health issues, such as anxiety and depression, can be exacerbated by poor indoor air quality. Constant exposure to allergens and irritants may contribute to mood disorders and decreased quality of life.

Addressing these hidden dangers requires a multifaceted approach. Regular cleaning, including HEPA filtration and frequent vacuuming, can reduce pet-related particulates. Proper ventilation systems help maintain air quality, even in sealed homes.

Grooming pets and keeping them out of bedrooms can minimize allergen spread. Air purifiers designed to capture pet dander and associated pollutants provide additional protection. Maintaining optimal humidity levels discourages dust mite proliferation.

Understanding the risks of indoor pet ownership is needed for making informed decisions. While pets provide companionship, they can also impact health and air quality. Regular health check-ups for pets and humans and strategies to maintain a healthy home enable responsible pet ownership.

Chapter 4

Parasites and Worms from Dogs

Dogs can transmit various parasites and worms to humans, posing health risks. Typical dog parasites include roundworms, hookworms, tapeworms, and giardia. These organisms can enter the human body through different routes, usually involving contact with contaminated soil or feces.

Roundworms, such as Toxocara canis, enter humans by ingesting eggs found in the soil. Hookworms can penetrate the skin when walking barefoot on contaminated ground. Tapeworms may enter the body if humans ingest infected fleas.

Transmission can occur through handling dog feces without proper hygiene, allowing dogs to lick faces, and sharing sleeping spaces. These behaviors increase the risk of parasite transfer from dogs to humans, and close contact with infected dogs raises the likelihood of exposure.

The health impacts vary depending on the specific organism and the severity of the infection. Roundworms can cause visceral larva migrans, affecting organs like the liver and lungs. Hookworms can lead to cutaneous larva migrans, causing skin irritation and itching. Tapeworms can cause gastrointestinal issues and nutrient deficiencies in humans. Giardia infections result in diarrhea, abdominal cramps, and nausea. Some parasites can cause more severe complications in individuals with weakened immune systems.

These infections can affect human health, leading to discomfort, fatigue, and potential long-term consequences. Financial impacts include medical expenses for diagnosis and treatment. Productivity may decrease due to illness-related absences from work or school.

Treatment involves antiparasitic medications prescribed by healthcare professionals. Proper hygiene practices and environmental sanitation are needed to eliminate parasites. Follow-up tests ensure complete eradication of the organisms. To limit parasites, dogs must be dewormed regularly. Wash hands after handling pets or their waste. Avoid walking barefoot in areas where dogs defecate.

Keep living spaces clean and vacuum them to remove potential parasite eggs. Prevent dogs from licking faces or sharing beds with humans. Immediately clean up dog feces in yards and public areas.

Educate children about proper hygiene practices when interacting with pets. Inspect dogs for signs of parasites and seek veterinary care if symptoms appear. Maintain clean environments to reduce the risk of parasite transmission.

Chapter 5

Cats and Toxoplasma Gondii

Toxoplasma gondii infects rats, making them attracted to cat urine. When cats interact with infected rats, they become hosts. The parasite thrives in cats and is excreted through feces, often in litter boxes.

Physicians advise pregnant women to avoid cat litter boxes due to T. gondii infection risks. Early pregnancy infections can cause miscarriages or stillbirths. Second-trimester infections may lead to hydrocephalus, microcephaly, or developmental delays. Third-trimester infections have high transmission rates but often result in asymptomatic infants with potential later complications.

An estimated 30% of cats in the USA carry T. gondii parasites. Over 40 million people in the U.S. are infected with toxoplasmosis. Primary transmission routes include ingesting undercooked meat, contaminated water, and contact with cat feces.

T. gondii affects men and women differently. In men, it may increase testosterone levels and risk-taking behaviors. Women may experience personality changes, increased extroversion, and conscientiousness. The parasite can influence human behavior, impacting intelligence, reaction time, and decision-making processes.

Immunocompromised individuals may experience severe symptoms like encephalitis, confusion, and vision problems. Diagnosis involves serological tests, PCR tests, and imaging. Treatment includes antiparasitic drugs like pyrimethamine and sulfadiazine, along with folinic acid.

If you are infected with T. gondii, consult healthcare professionals for proper diagnosis and treatment. To avoid infection, practice good hygiene, cook meat, and wash fruits and vegetables. Responsible pet ownership and hygiene practices can also reduce risks.

Chapter 6

Zoonotic Diseases

Household animals can transmit various zoonotic diseases to humans. Rabies, toxoplasmosis, salmonellosis, campylobacteriosis, giardiasis, and ringworm are among the diseases spread by pets. These illnesses are transmitted through bites, scratches, or exposure to animal waste and fluids.

Rabies is a viral infection spread through bites from infected animals. It affects the nervous system, causing fever, headache, and confusion, and can lead to paralysis and death if untreated. Immediate medical attention and post-exposure prevention are essential for survival. Animal vaccination can prevent rabies transmission.

Toxoplasma gondii causes toxoplasmosis and spreads through contact with cat waste. It causes flu-like symptoms in healthy individuals but can be a risk factor for pregnant women and immunocompromised people. Treatment involves antiparasitic medications. Proper hygiene and avoiding contact with litter during pregnancy reduce risks.

Salmonellosis and campylobacteriosis are bacterial infections spread through contaminated waste or undercooked meat. They cause gastrointestinal symptoms like diarrhea, fever, and abdominal pain. Treatment involves hydration and, in severe cases, antibiotics. Proper food handling and hygiene help prevent transmission.

Giardiasis, caused by Giardia, spreads through contaminated water or contact with infected waste. It causes diarrhea, abdominal cramps, and nausea. Treatment includes antiparasitic medications. Proper hygiene and avoiding contaminated water sources reduce transmission risks.

As stated earlier in the book, ringworm is a fungal infection spread through direct contact with infected animals. It causes circular, red, itchy patches on the skin. Antifungal medications treat the disease. Regular grooming and veterinary check-ups help prevent its spread.

Preventing zoonotic diseases involves proper animal care, regular veterinary check-ups, and good hygiene practices. Washing hands after handling animals, cleaning waste areas, and avoiding contact with animal waste reduce transmission risks. Keeping animals vaccinated and dewormed also helps prevent disease spread.

Immunocompromised individuals, pregnant women, young children, and the elderly should take extra precautions when interacting with animals. They should avoid direct contact with animal waste and bodily fluids. Regular veterinary care and prompt treatment of animal illnesses further reduce zoonotic disease risks.

While household animals pose some zoonotic risks, exotic pets, and wildlife introduce additional concerns. Reptiles, amphibians, and insects can carry unique pathogens unfamiliar to owners. The next chapter explores zoonotic diseases associated with these less common animals.

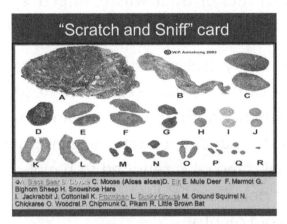

Chapter 7

Wildlife and Health: The Hidden Dangers in Our Homes

Rodents and small mammals impact indoor air quality and health. Mouse urine protein, an allergen, aerosolizes, causing respiratory issues. Contaminated spaces harbor bacteria like Salmonella, posing illness risks. Mice damaged appliances and furniture, sparking electrical fires. Proper prevention measures, such as sealing cracks and storing food, can reduce these risks.

Rats spread diseases like Hantavirus and salmonellosis, posing health risks. Symptoms include fatigue, fever, and breathing difficulties. Transmission occurs through contact with rats or their waste. Effective control includes sealing entry points and maintaining cleanliness.

Brown bats are typical in North America. They consume insects but can carry diseases. White-nose syndrome endangers them, causing weight loss and death. Bats hibernate in caves and attics, returning in spring to roost. Professional removal is required to handle guano and prevent air pollution. Sealing entry points is needed in order to avoid reentry.

Raccoons enter homes through roof openings, causing damage and health risks. These furry night crawlers transmit rabies and parasites through their feces. Professional removal and cleanup are recommended. Squirrels cause power outages and damage homes. These tight-rope-tailed creatures chew through materials, leading to leaks and flooding. Professional cleanup is advised due to disease risks.

Birds, including parrots, impact indoor air quality. Dust, dander, and bird droppings accumulate in cages, irritating respiratory systems. Psittacosis, parrot fever, is transmitted from birds to humans, causing flu-like symptoms and pneumonia. Maintaining clean environments and ensuring proper ventilation is important to prevent these health issues.

When not maintained, household aquariums can harbor harmful bacteria. Mycobacterium marinum, found in aquariums, causes skin infections known as fish tank granuloma. Contaminated water can lead to bacterial infections if it contacts open wounds. Regular cleaning and proper hygiene practices are needed to prevent illness.

Exotic pets like monkeys, wildlife felines, and other wild animals can be dangerous and transmit diseases. Monkeys may carry the Herpes B virus, while wildlife felines pose physical threats. These animals require specialized care and environments, which are difficult to replicate in homes. This wildlife belongs in the wild, not in domestic settings.

Chapter 8

The Economic Burden of Pet Ownership

Owning a pet brings financial responsibilities that accumulate over time. The initial purchase or adoption fees are small compared to the long-term costs that stretch for years. Pet ownership involves daily, monthly, and yearly expenses necessary to maintain the pet's health and well-being. Over a lifetime, these costs can amount to a significant financial burden for pet owners.

The annual costs of owning a dog or cat can vary, but food is a primary expense for both. Depending on the size and diet of the dog, dog food costs between $250 and $700 annually. Cat food, requiring less food, ranges from $150 to $500 annually. Pet food alone can cost thousands of dollars over a pet's lifetime, but that's only part of the equation.

Regular grooming is another needed expense, with dog grooming ranging from $30 to $90 per visit. Cats groom themselves but may need professional help, costing around $50. Accessories like beds, toys, leashes, and litter boxes can add up to $100 to $200 annually.

Medical care is one of the most expensive aspects of pet ownership. Depending on the pet's location, routine annual check-ups and vaccinations cost between $200 and $500. Medications are common in pets as they age. Medications for allergies, arthritis, or chronic pain can cost between $20 and $100 monthly. Daily medication for conditions like heartworm, diabetes, or thyroid issues can increase over a pet's life. Depending on the complexity, if a dog requires surgery, such as removing a tumor or fixing a broken bone, costs can reach between $1,500 and $5,000.

As a pet owner, the time investment is as significant as the financial one. A dog owner spends time walking the dog, feeding it, and playing with it. Walking alone can take up to 30 minutes to an hour a day, up to over 365 hours a year. Feeding a pet takes less time but is a daily routine, taking up at least 10 minutes daily for feeding and cleaning up. Depending on the pet's age, veterinary visits add hours monthly or yearly. If one lives to 80, thousands of hours are spent on pet care, feeding, and companionship over a lifetime of pet ownership.

Beyond the financial and time costs, there are significant opportunity costs to consider in pet ownership. The money spent on pet food, grooming, and medical care could be used for other important causes. For instance, the money could go toward helping the homeless or caring for elderly family members, reducing their need to enter nursing homes. Volunteering at nonprofits focusing on environmental or humanitarian causes becomes a missed opportunity. Owning a pet may limit the time to write books, pursue a garden, or engage in other personal pursuits that contribute to personal growth.

Pet ownership often limits personal freedom. If you have a dog at home, you must plan around its needs. This can restrict travel plans or spontaneous outings, forcing you to rush home to walk or feed the dog. Staying out late, attending events, or spending nights at friends' becomes more complicated when your pet depends on you. You may even drive home to care for the pet, risking traffic tickets and stress. Without a pet, enjoying extended vacations or more time with friends and family becomes easier without being tied to a routine.

Pet ownership brings joy and companionship but comes at the cost of time, money, and personal freedom. As rewarding as it can be, it is necessary to recognize the substantial commitment and opportunity costs involved. Pet owners invest thousands of dollars in a pet's life and dedicate hours to caring for their furry companions. For some, the joy of having a pet outweighs these costs, but for others, the trade-offs may be too significant.

Chapter 9

Pets and Stress

Stress is a state of mental or emotional strain resulting from demanding circumstances. It is a leading cause of various issues worldwide. Stress contributes to ailments like heart disease, diabetes, and depression, which lead to numerous deaths daily. Chronic tension can trigger heart attacks, blood clots, and aneurysms by causing prolonged inflammation and high blood pressure.

People experience strain due to overwhelming responsibilities, excessive tasks, and insufficient time. Unpredictable events, like financial setbacks or bad luck, can also heighten anxiety levels. The pressure to balance work, family, and personal life often makes individuals anxious and exhausted. This relentless cycle can have severe implications for well-being.

While pets are often a source of comfort, they can also be stressors. Behavioral issues, such as aggression or excessive barking, can cause tension. Problems in animals, like chronic illnesses, can lead to financial strain and emotional distress. The death of a pet can result in profound grief and depression, further exacerbating anxiety.

Owning pets involves responsibilities that can add to daily stress. Rushing home to care for an animal can be stressful, mainly if unexpected delays occur. Animal-related accidents, such as dog bites or car accidents while hurrying home, can have serious consequences, leading to increased anxiety and risks to well-being.

Chronic tension weakens the immune system, making individuals more susceptible to illnesses. A compromised immune system can lead to frequent infections, prolonged recovery, and increased disease vulnerability. The cumulative effect on the body can result in difficulties in well-being.

To maintain health and longevity, it is important to manage stress effectively. Reducing tension may involve reconsidering pet ownership or coping with animal-related stressors. Simplifying life by limiting responsibilities can help alleviate strain. Embracing a balanced lifestyle can lead to improved well-being and a longer life.

Chapter 10

Dangerous Animals in the Home

Social media platforms like YouTube have distorted perceptions of wildlife, leading people to bring dangerous animals into their homes. Videos featuring lions, tigers, and alligators as companions create a false sense of safety and normalcy. However, these animals pose significant risks, such as a deer kicking a child. The allure of exotic pets can overshadow the inherent dangers they present.

Certain dog breeds are known for their aggressive tendencies, with pit bulls and Rottweilers often cited in attack statistics. In the United States, 4.5 million dog bites occur per year, with around 30 to 50 resulting in fatalities. These breeds have been involved in numerous incidents where owners or others have been harmed. Caretakers of aggressive dogs may face legal consequences, including imprisonment if their pet takes a life.

The United States is home to millions of dogs, with pit bulls and Rottweilers among the most common types of dogs involved in severe attacks. Owning hazardous pets requires specific insurance policies, often with high premiums. Many insurers exclude coverage for certain breeds or exotic creatures due to their risk. Without adequate insurance, owners might face financial ruin if their pet causes injury.

Depending on the breed and history, dog liability insurance can cost anywhere from $10 to over $1,000 per year. Legal and financial ramifications can include lawsuits that deplete life savings if a dog bite results in severe harm. The risks associated with owning dangerous animals often outweigh the perceived benefits. Therefore, legal liabilities, high insurance costs, and potential for injury should deter individuals from keeping such pets.

Real-life examples highlight the severe consequences of owning risky animals. Individuals have sometimes faced legal action or imprisonment due to their pets' actions. Animal hoarders or petting zoo owners have also encountered legal issues when wildlife harmed visitors. Understanding the potential consequences should temper the desire for exotic or aggressive pets.

Do we need this potential aggravation, stress, burden, or gamble that injury will not occur? The answer is no. Choosing safer, more manageable animals can prevent unnecessary harm. Responsible pet ownership involves understanding and mitigating the risks of keeping animals.

Chapter 11

The Future of Pet Ownership

Pet ownership is rising, with more families welcoming animals into their homes. In 2023, 66% of U.S. households owned pets, a significant increase from previous decades. This trend is expected to continue, with projections suggesting pet ownership will grow by 4% per year over the next 20 years. By 2043, an estimated 86% of households may own pets, reflecting a substantial demographic shift.

Globally, there are over a billion pets, with 900 million dogs and 600 million cats worldwide. Many people today choose pets as substitutes for human relationships or children. Various factors influence this trend, including changes in world views and personal preferences. Birth rates have declined globally, with Japan at 1.2, Europe at 1.4, and the USA at 1.7, far below the 2.2 needed to sustain a population.

Governments and social narratives may contribute to these trends, promoting pet ownership as an alternative to traditional family structures. The reasons behind these trends are complex and multifaceted, warranting a comprehensive exploration beyond the scope of this chapter.

Demographic shifts have led to more people living in shared spaces, often with pets. The COVID-19 pandemic accelerated this trend, with college students and young adults returning home and bringing their pets.

In California, regulations permit people to live in garages, reflecting the impact of the housing crisis. Rising rents and prices make owning a home unaffordable for many, leading to shared living arrangements. This shift has implications for household dynamics, urban planning, and community resources. As pet ownership increases, so does the demand for pet-related services and infrastructure.

The environmental impact of increased pet ownership is significant. Pet food production contributes to carbon emissions, with 106 million tons of CO_2 generated annually. The energy required to produce and transport pet food adds to the ecological footprint. Plastic waste from pet care, such as dog poop bags, also contributes to environmental degradation. These bags are often non-recyclable and end up in landfills, adding to plastic pollution. In 50,000 years, aliens might find dog DNA in garbage dumps alongside plastic poop bags.

Pet food manufacturing also generates substantial wastewater containing contaminants that can harm ecosystems. Effective treatment solutions are necessary to mitigate these impacts and comply with environmental regulations. The industry's ecological footprint includes greenhouse gas emissions, water usage, and waste production. These factors contribute to climate change and demand sustainable practices.

The global pet industry produces 64 million tons of CO_2 annually, and pet food manufacturing alone uses significant water resources. Pet ownership's environmental impact has a secondary effect on climate change, which is more important than stopping coal or oil consumption.

Owning pets may soon involve additional financial considerations, such as license fees and carbon credit taxes. Some countries have already implemented carbon taxes, which affect pet owners' expenses. As environmental awareness grows, policies may evolve to address pets' ecological impact. This could lead to higher costs and stricter regulations for pet owners.

The decision to own pets involves weighing the benefits against the responsibilities and potential difficulties. While pets offer companionship and emotional support, they also require care, attention, and resources. As society evolves, so will the dynamics of pet ownership, which are shaped by cultural, economic, and environmental factors.

Pets can harm both people and the earth. Their presence in homes affects human relationships, environmental sustainability, and financial stability. Understanding these impacts is essential for making informed decisions about pet ownership.

Chapter 12

Health Implications of Changing Homes along with Modern Pet Ownership

In today's world, homes are increasingly insulated, reducing air exchange. This shift began during the energy crises, prompting tighter construction to conserve energy. As construction costs escalate, homes become more compact and diverse, with many opting for tiny homes, trailers, or vans. Living in confined spaces with pets, like two people and a dog in a small truck, may harm health.

Even those experiencing homelessness are acquiring pets despite struggling to care for themselves. The presence of pets in these situations raises concerns about adequate care and living conditions. Another issue is pet hoarding, where individuals keep multiple animals in small spaces, creating unhealthy environments. Homes with six cats, six litter boxes, or four dogs with children often reek of urine and ammonia, both unhealthy.

The environmental impact of pets extends beyond indoor spaces. Trees in urban areas suffer damage from dogs marking their territory, which is evident in the bark erosion at tree bases. Observing neighborhood walks reveals the extent of this damage. HVAC systems accumulate pet-related contaminants inside homes, including dander, saliva, and hair, leading to bio-growth and mold.

Tight living spaces and high indoor humidity exacerbate mold growth, posing health risks. Mold thrives in these environments, potentially making residents sick, mainly when pets contribute to humidity and CO_2 levels. Mold has significant health implications, affecting respiratory health and overall well-being.

Comparing Western children's health to global averages reveals a concerning trend. The United States, with a high pet ownership rate, also reports increased asthma cases among children. Studies suggest a link between pet ownership and respiratory issues, with more pets correlating to higher asthma prevalence. This connection underscores the need for awareness of the health impacts of modern pet ownership.

As homes become smaller and more insulated, pets' presence introduces new health risks, from mold growth to respiratory issues.

Chapter 13

Psychological Effects of Pet Ownership

The surge in mental health issues is driven by political, religious, racial, gender, and vaccination status divisions. Family gatherings are sparse, while news outlets bombard us with harmful, agenda-driven content. Children face developmental issues due to exposure to pesticides, chemicals, GMOs, and radiation. As a result, emotional support animals have become a common coping mechanism.

Instead of seeking human connections, many individuals turn to pets for companionship and emotional support. Emotional support animals accompany their owners in various settings, including stores and airplanes. However, their presence can create discomfort for others. For example, a barking dog on a plane can cause passengers to sneeze. The focus on accommodating emotional support animals often overlooks the well-being of others in shared spaces.

The rise in emotional support animals impacts rental markets, with landlords facing potential property damage. Landlords cannot refuse tenants with emotional support animals if the property has a no-pets policy. This can lead to overcrowded living situations, as seen in my Airbnb experience with three guests and their three emotional support dogs. After I informed them of potential cleanup costs, they canceled their reservation.

Dependency on emotional support animals raises concerns about reliance on pets for emotional stability. The number of emotional support animals has surged since 2000. Today, in 2024, millions of emotional support animals exist in the United States, with numbers increasing yearly. This trend suggests a growing dependency on animals for mental health support.

Projections indicate the number of emotional support animals will continue to rise over the next 20 years. This increase reflects a shift in how people address mental health issues, often at the expense of traditional social interactions. Relying on pets for emotional support can lead to potential dependency issues, as individuals may struggle to cope without their animals.

The impact on social interactions and relationships is significant, as people turn to animals for companionship. This shift affects how individuals form connections and engage with others, leading to isolation.

Chapter 14

The Perpetual Toddler: Life with Pets

Living with dogs and cats is like living with a 2-year-old child in several ways. The emotional toll of constant attention, supervision, and care throughout the day is important. They need regular feeding, bathroom breaks, and exercise, much like toddlers. Pets often seek attention and playtime, interrupting daily activities or work.

They can be messy, leaving toys scattered and occasionally having accidents in the house. Owners must teach pets where to go to the bathroom, where to eat, and when to stop unwanted behaviors like barking or scratching furniture. It's a constant battle; some pets annoy their owners with their persistent need for attention. Owners are constantly on edge, unsure what their pets might do next. Unlike a human child, this state of dependency never ends with pets.

The "2-year-old" phase lasts throughout their life until they pass away. A human child would outgrow this stage in a few years, becoming more intelligent and self-sufficient. Pets, however, remain at a similar cognitive level, requiring constant care and attention for their entire lifespan. This continuous care can cause anxiety and stress for pet owners. The relentless need for attention, feeding, exercise, and cleanup can be overwhelming. It's a form of self-imposed slavery, as owners are perpetually tied to their pets' needs.

They must plan their lives around their animals, limiting travel, social activities, and personal freedom. The responsibility of caring for a perpetual "2-year-old" can be emotionally and physically draining, creating a sense of being trapped in a never-ending cycle of caregiving. Pet owners often become borderline control freaks, constantly scolding their pets and rewarding good behavior with treats or toys. This dynamic creates a power imbalance where the owner controls the pet's life completely.

Pets are confined and have limited freedom except for designated walking or bathroom times in the backyard. Modern technology extends this control further. Many owners now use tracking devices and cameras to monitor their pets, transforming into police officers surveilling their animals. This constant monitoring adds another layer of stress and responsibility to pet ownership, blurring the lines between care and obsessive control.

Pet owners essentially live with perpetual two-year-olds, becoming slaves to their pets' needs while simultaneously transforming into police officers and control freaks. This dynamic creates an unbalanced relationship where the owner controls every aspect of the pet's life. In a human relationship, such controlling behavior would likely lead to the partner leaving. However, pets cannot escape this situation, remaining dependent on their owners for life. Training and teaching a "two-year-old" for decades can become tiresome, tedious, and time-consuming. Other opportunities and aspects of life often go by the wayside as pet owners dedicate significant time and energy to their animals.

This raises the question: Is having pets truly what we want, or have these desires been programmed into our psyche through mainstream narratives, social engineering, or propaganda? The pervasive promotion of pet ownership in media and society may have shaped our perceptions, leading us to accept this demanding lifestyle as usual or desirable.

Chapter 15

Final Words

Rethinking Pet OwnershipPet ownership burdens society with health risks and environmental damage. Alternative models emerge but fail to address core issues of animal dependency.

Pet-sharing programs create inconsistent care and stress for animals. Fostering initiatives lead to emotional attachment and rehoming difficulties.

Community animal spaces spread diseases among visitors. They provide fleeting interactions that fail to satisfy emotional needs. These programs serve as band-aids for pet obsession. Environmental concerns reveal the unsustainability of widespread pet ownership.

Pet food production depletes resources and contributes to climate change. Animal waste pollutes waterways and spreads bacteria in urban areas. "Sustainable" pet care practices greenwash a destructive industry. Public health policies struggle to contain dangers posed by domestic animals.

Zoonotic diseases emerge from pet populations. Vaccination requirements prove inadequate in preventing outbreaks. Animal control measures strain public resources and result in euthanasia. Indoor air quality suffers in pet-owning households. New ways to connect with animals without full-time commitment are emerging. In Japan, cat cafes allow visitors to enjoy feline company for hourly fees. Some European countries offer dog-sharing apps, connecting owners with temporary caretakers.

Municipalities create spaces for animal interaction without ownership. These areas cater to those seeking animal companionship without long-term responsibilities.

People recognize the environmental impact of pets, from food production to waste management.

Companies develop sustainable pet products to address ecological concerns. Health issues related to pet ownership gain attention. Air quality in pet-friendly homes becomes problematic, prompting the use of HEPA vacuums and air purifiers.

Pets are involved in mental health treatment. Laws increasingly view animals as family members rather than property. Technology enables pet health tracking and virtual vet visits. Schools teach animal care and welfare.

My daughter pleaded against writing this book, but I felt compelled. The idea of carbon-taxing pets is a necessary conversation. As society reduces coal, oil, and meat consumption, we must consider all carbon footprint contributors.

When my daughter questioned her cat's environmental impact, I explained the collective effect of millions of pets. She left, unconvinced or uninterested. Pet owners might avoid this book, unwilling to confront environmental implications.

Those without pets might dismiss it as irrelevant. I imagine this book, discarded among dog waste bags, discovered by future archaeologists. It may serve as a testament to humans' curious choices on Earth.

Chapter 16

Bibligrapjuy

Chapter 1: The Evolution of Pet Ownership

1. Grier, K. C. (2006). Pets in America: A History. University of North Carolina Press.

2. Herzog, H. (2010). Some We Love, Some We Hate, Some We Eat: Why It's So Hard to Think Straight About Animals. Harper.

3. Serpell, J. (1996). In the Company of Animals: A Study of Human-Animal Relationships. Cambridge University Press.

4. American Veterinary Medical Association. (2017-2018). U.S. Pet Ownership & Demographics Sourcebook.

5. Bradshaw, J. (2017). The Animals Among Us: How Pets Make Us Human. Basic Books.

6. Vovk, M. (2023). Fix Your Toxic Home and Live Longer. Self-published.

7. Pet Food Institute. (2024). Pet Ownership Statistics.

8. Centers for Disease Control and Prevention. (2023). Healthy Pets, Healthy People.

9. American Pet Products Association. (2024). National Pet Owners Survey.

10. World Health Organization. (2022). Zoonoses.

11. Forbes Advisor. (2024). Pet Ownership Statistics 2024.

12. American Veterinary Medical Association. (2022). U.S. pet ownership statistics.

13. Wellbeing International Studies Repository. (n.d.). Companion Animal Statistics in the USA.

14. Statista. (2024). Pet ownership in the U.S. - statistics & facts.

15. National Center for Biotechnology Information. (2018). Dog Population & Dog Sheltering Trends in the United States.

16. Wikipedia. (n.d.). Dogs in the United States.

17. Insurance Information Institute. (n.d.). Facts + Statistics: Pet Ownership and Insurance.

18. City of Aurora. (n.d.). Population.

19. Vovk, Marko. (n.d.). Fix Your Toxic Home and Live Longer.

Chapter 2: The Rise of Indoor Pets

1. American Pet Products Association. (2024). 2023-2024 APPA National Pet Owners Survey.

2. American Veterinary Medical Association. (2022). U.S. pet ownership statistics.

3. Forbes Advisor. (2024). Pet Ownership Statistics 2024.

4. Pawlicy. (2024). Pet Ownership Statistics by State.

5. Statista. (2024). Pet ownership in the U.S. - statistics & facts.

6. Vovk, Marko. (n.d.). Fix Your Toxic Home and Live Longer.

7. Wellbeing International Studies Repository. (n.d.). Companion Animal Statistics in the USA.

Chapter 3: The Hidden Dangers of Indoor Pets

1. American Lung Association. (2024). Asthma and Children Fact Sheet.

2. Centers for Disease Control and Prevention. (2023). Asthma Surveillance Data.

3. Environmental Protection Agency. (2024). Indoor Air Quality in Homes.

4. Journal of Allergy and Clinical Immunology. (2022). Trends in Allergy Prevalence.

5. National Institutes of Health. (2023). Dust Mite Allergens and Human Health.

6. World Health Organization. (2024). Household Air Pollution and Health.

7. American Academy of Allergy, Asthma & Immunology. (2023). Pet Allergies.

8. Journal of Environmental Health. (2021). Indoor Air Quality in Energy-Efficient Homes.

9. Vovk, Marko. (n.d.). Fix Your Toxic Home and Live Longer.

Chapter 4: Parasites and Worms from Dogs

1. Centers for Disease Control and Prevention. (2021). Parasites - Zoonotic Hookworm.

2. Companion Animal Parasite Council. (2022). Guidelines for Controlling Internal and External Parasites in U.S. Dogs and Cats.

3. European Scientific Counsel Companion Animal Parasites. (2020). Worm Control in Dogs and Cats.

4. Macpherson, C. N. L. (2013). The epidemiology and public health importance of toxocariasis: A zoonosis of global importance. International Journal for Parasitology, 43(12-13), 999-1008.

5. Robertson, I. D., & Thompson, R. C. (2002). Enteric parasitic zoonoses of domesticated dogs and cats. Microbes and Infection, 4(8), 867-873.

6. American Veterinary Medical Association. (2004). U.S. pet ownership & demographics sourcebook.

7. Merck Veterinary Manual. (2023). Gastrointestinal Parasites of Dogs.

8. Schantz, P.M. (1989). Toxocara larva migrans now. American Journal of Tropical Medicine and Hygiene.

Chapter 5: Cats and Toxoplasma Gondii

1. Centers for Disease Control and Prevention. (2022). Toxoplasmosis.

2. Dubey, J. P. (2020). Toxoplasmosis of Animals and Humans. CRC Press.

3. Flegr, J. (2013). How and why Toxoplasma makes us crazy. Trends in Parasitology, 29(4), 156-163.

4. Jones, J. L., et al. (2018). Toxoplasma gondii infection in the United States, 2011-2014. American Journal of Tropical Medicine and Hygiene, 98(2), 551-557.

5. Lafferty, K. D. (2006). Can the common brain parasite, Toxoplasma gondii, influence human culture? Proceedings of the Royal Society B: Biological Sciences, 273(1602), 2749-2755.

6. Robert-Gangneux, F., & Dardé, M. L. (2012). Epidemiology of and diagnostic strategies for toxoplasmosis. Clinical Microbiology Reviews, 25(2), 264-296.

Chapter 6 & 7: Zoonotic Diseases & Wildlife and Health

1. Environmental Health Perspectives. (n.d.). Indoor Air Quality and Health Risks of Rodents.

2. Centers for Disease Control and Prevention. (n.d.). Rodent Control and Prevention.

3. Journal of Wildlife Diseases. (n.d.). Bats and Disease Transmission.

4. Wildlife Society Bulletin. (n.d.). Raccoons: Damage and Disease Risks.

5. IEEE Transactions on Power Delivery. (n.d.). Squirrels and Electrical Outages.

6. Journal of Urban Health. (n.d.). Pigeon-Related Health Risks.

7. Canadian Journal of Zoology. (n.d.). Skunk Behavior and Disease.

8. Journal of Pest Science. (n.d.). Groundhog and Structural Damage.

9. Australian Mammalogy. (n.d.). Possum Behavior and Health Implications.

10. Disease Outbreak Control Division. (n.d.). Psittacosis (Ornithosis, Parrot Fever).

11. VCA Animal Hospitals. (n.d.). Common Diseases of Pet Snakes.

12. Worms & Germs Blog. (n.d.). Zoonotic Infection From A Household Aquarium.

13. Born Free USA. (n.d.). The Dangers of Keeping Exotic Pets.

Chapter 8: The Economic Burden of Pet Ownership

1. American Veterinary Medical Association. (2021). Pet Ownership and Spending Statistics.

2. ASPCA. (2022). The True Costs of Pet Ownership.

3. Petfinder. (2023). Average Costs of Owning a Pet.

4. VetInfo. (2021). Cost of Pet Medications and Surgery.

Chapter 9: Pets and Stress

1. National Center for Biotechnology Information. (n.d.). Current Directions in Stress and Human

Immune Function.

2. Sandia Animal Clinic. (n.d.). Stress and Our Pets: Causes, Effects, and Prevention.

3. PubMed. (n.d.). Effects of stress on immune function: the good, the bad.

4. Merriam-Webster. (n.d.). Stress Definition & Meaning.

5. National Center for Biotechnology Information. (n.d.). Daily exposure to stressors, daily perceived severity of stress, and mortality.

6. MedlinePlus. (n.d.). Stress and your health.

7. Mayo Clinic Health System. (n.d.). 5 Tips to Manage Stress.

8. American Heart Association. (n.d.). Chronic stress can cause heart trouble.

9. World Health Organization. (n.d.). Stress.

10. Manhattan Cardiology. (n.d.). How does stress affect your heart?

11. McLean Hospital. (n.d.). Do You Manage Your Time Well?

12. NIH News in Health. (n.d.). The Power of Pets.

13. Mayo Clinic. (n.d.). Chronic stress puts your health at risk.

14. URMC Rochester. (n.d.). Stress Can Increase Your Risk for Heart Disease.

Chapter 10: Dangerous Animals in the Home

1. Fatal Dog Attacks. (n.d.). Fatal Dog Attacks in the U.S. — Breeds, Statistics, & Studies.

2. Landlord.com. (n.d.). Dangerous or Vicious Animals By State.

3. Animal Legal & Historical Center. (n.d.). Detailed Discussion Landowner and Landlord Liability for Dangerous Animals.

4. Dog Bite Law. (n.d.). Force Dog Owners to Have Insurance That Would Compensate Dog Bite Victims.

5. J&Y Law Firm. (n.d.). Dog Bite Statistics by Breed.

6. Dog Bite Law. (n.d.). Where to Get Dog Owner Liability Insurance.

7. Animal Legal & Historical Center. (n.d.). Exotic Pet

Laws.

8. Ndakotalaw.com. (n.d.). The Legal and Financial Consequences of a Catastrophic Dog Bite.

9. Goldberg & Loren Law Firm. (n.d.). Top 20 Dog Bite Statistics for 2023.

10. National Association of Realtors. (n.d.). What If the Home Sellers Have a Dangerous Pet?

11. Bankrate. (n.d.). Dog Breeds That Affect Your Insurance Coverage.

12. DogsBite.org. (n.d.). U.S. Dog Bite Fatalities - Dog Bite Statistics.

13. MKP Law Group. (n.d.). 25+ Important Dog Bite Statistics & Bites by Breed for 2024.

14. Wikipedia. (n.d.). Fatal Dog Attacks in the United States.

15. Safer Pets. (n.d.). Top Injuries Caused by Animals Around the World.

16. DogsBite.org. (n.d.). Dangerous Dog Breeds.

Chapter 11: The Future of Pet Ownership

1. All About Feed. (n.d.). Sustainable pet food pro-

duction in the US.

2. Pet Food Processing. (n.d.). Pet Food Conference report: The true impact of pets.

3. MacroTrends. (n.d.). Japan Birth Rate 1950-2024.

4. Nippon.com. (n.d.). Number of Births in Japan Reaches New Low in 2023.

5. American Pet Products Association. (n.d.). Pet Ownership Statistics, Pet Industry Trends & Pet Research by APPA.

6. Dogster. (n.d.). Pet Industry Statistics 2024: Facts & Trends.

7. Recovery Realty. (n.d.). Pet Ownership Statistics – Latest Numbers and Trends in 2024.

8. The Zebra. (n.d.). Pet Ownership Statistics in 2024.

9. World Bank. (n.d.). State and Trends of Carbon Pricing 2024.

10. PubMed. (n.d.). Dog poop bags: A non-negligible source of plastic pollution.

11. Earth.org. (n.d.). The Environmental Impact of

Pets: Working Towards Sustainable.

12. Pets and Housing. (n.d.). Affordability and Pets: Rising Costs Forcing Tough Decisions.

13. HealthforAnimals. (n.d.). Global Trends in the Pet Population.

14. Simply Insurance. (n.d.). How Many Pets Are In The World & The US? 71+ Pet Stats.

Chapter 12: Health Implications of Changing Homes along with Modern Pet Ownership

1. National Center for Biotechnology Information. (n.d.). Current pet ownership modifies the adverse association between ambient air pollution and asthma in children. PMC8099301.

2. PubMed. (n.d.). Associations of early-life pet ownership with asthma and allergic outcomes. 35150722.

3. National Center for Biotechnology Information. (n.d.). The relationship of domestic pet ownership with the risk of childhood asthma. PMC9352935.

4. PLOS ONE. (n.d.). Does Pet Ownership in Infancy Lead to Asthma or Allergy at School Age? 10.1371/journal.pone.0043214.

5. National Center for Biotechnology Information. (n.d.). Pet's influence on humans' daily physical activity and mental health. PMC10262044.

6. Dogster. (n.d.). 20 Global Pet Ownership Statistics to Know in 2024.

7. MarketWatch. (n.d.). Top Pet Ownership Statistics and Facts (2024).

8. Population Association of America. (n.d.). Pet Ownership and Access as Predictors of Self-Reported Health in a National Sample of U.S. Elders. paa2015.populationassociation.org.

Chapter 13: Psychological Effects of Pet Ownership

1. National Center for Biotechnology Information. (2018). Dog Population & Dog Sheltering Trends in the United States.

2. Population Association of America. (2015). Pet Ownership and Access as Predictors of Self-Reported Health in a National Sample of U.S. Elders.

3. National Center for Biotechnology Information. (2024). Pet's influence on humans' daily physical activity and mental health: a meta-analysis.

4. CertaPet. (2018). Newly Released Study Reveals

Health Benefits of Emotional Support Animals.

5. The Zebra. (2024). Animal Therapy Statistics in 2024.

Chapter 14: The Perpetual Toddler: Life with Pets

1. Brooks, H. L., Rushton, K., Lovell, K., Bee, P., Walker, L., Grant, L., & Rogers, A. (2018). The power of support from companion animals for people living with mental health problems: a systematic review and narrative synthesis of the evidence. BMC psychiatry, 18(1), 31.

2. Westgarth, C., Christley, R. M., Marvin, G., & Perkins, E. (2019). The responsible dog owner: The construction of responsibility. Anthrozoös, 32(5), 631-646.

3. Purewal, R., Christley, R., Kordas, K., Joinson, C., Meints, K., Gee, N., & Westgarth, C. (2017). Companion animals and child/adolescent development: a systematic review of the evidence. International journal of environmental research and public health, 14(3), 234.

4. Hawkins, R. D., & Williams, J. M. (2017). Childhood attachment to pets: Associations between pet attachment, attitudes to animals, compassion, and

humane behaviour. International journal of environmental research and public health, 14(5), 490.

Chapter 15, 16, 17: Beyond Ownership: Exploring New Models of Companionship

1. BMC Psychiatry. (2018). The power of support from companion animals for people living with...

2. Scientific Reports. (2022). Environmental impact of diets for dogs and cats.

3. LinkedIn. (2023). Public awareness about pets.

4. NCBI. (2022). Associations between Pet Care Responsibility, Companion Animal...

5. University of Edinburgh. (2023). Behind the environmental impacts of pet foods.

6. FOUR PAWS in US. (2023). Responsible Pet Ownership Program.

7. Frontiers in Veterinary Science.

Made in the USA
Middletown, DE
20 October 2024